Are Revenue Sharing Article/Content Publishing Sites Beneficial?

By: James M. Lowrance © 2011

SECTION ONE

Legitimate Opportunities for Authors

To all of the sincere, hard-working authors and content contributors who are simply looking for honest websites to enter into successful, long-term relationship with.

TABLE OF CONTENTS (SECTION ONE):

INTRODUCTION:

The revenue-sharing content website industry has grown into a multi-billion dollar a year online business. These are websites (sites) that offer interesting or needed information to readers who visit their online pages but who at the same time, sell advertising units, which appear as ads around each piece of content they display (i.e. articles, audios, photos or videos).

In many cases these ads are the Google Adsense type. If authors or content contributors want to share in the revenue generated by these type sites they can register for an Adsense account and they will be supplied with their own unique account number, once approved. This allows Google to track the clicks on ads displayed around content they have submitted to websites and to be paid their percent of the revenue advertisers pay for those clicks on ads purchased by them. It is an effective and precise method of offering advertising online and to pay both the administration and content contributors at revenue-sharing websites. (NOTE: Google has strict policy against "click fraud" and they are well-equipped to track down unlawfully gained Adsense revenue.)

5

Some websites pay their contributors based on the numbers of clicks their content receives, rather than for numbers of clicks on ad-units and this can be something like $1.50 or $2.00 per 1,000 page-views on their combined pieces of content or paid on each individual piece of content that reaches this many page-views. Contributors are usually asked to provide a bank account for direct deposit of payments to them or they are asked to obtain a PayPal account for earned revenue deposits to be paid into. Other sites pay upfront amounts for content they accept from contributors or a combination of upfront payments and ongoing ad revenue shares. Yet other sites actually pay base salaries to their contributors, who in this case are often referred to as "Editors" or "Guides".

This system can be very beneficial to content contributors but much of this depends on what websites one decides to register-with and the level of quality content submissions one has. In some cases, less-reputable or dishonest revenue sharing websites have done disservice to their contributors, by discontinuing revenue-sharing after gleaning massive amounts of content from them.

They have also done a disservice by canceling contributor's memberships for bogus reasons or by unrightfully penalizing the revenue shares of members.

In the chapters that follow, I will address these types of issues and offer recommendations for choosing revenue sharing sites that can be beneficial rather than negative experiences for content contributors.

CHAPTER ONE

My Personal Experience with Revenue Sharing Websites

Beginning in year 2004, I began to write articles online, submitting them to websites that did not offer revenue share opportunities. I however, enjoyed these sites personally and felt that they offered high quality content to readers. My main enjoyment of writing was to share helpful information to readers. In my case, being a medical patient, diagnosed with autoimmune thyroid disease and other co-morbid health disorders, I simply enjoyed sharing any knowledge I was gaining from extensive online searches, with fellow patients.

After a couple of years however, I became interested in submitting articles to revenue sharing sites. I felt that with the fact that visitors could still read articles at no charge and that advertisers actually benefited from this type set up, as well as the sites and content contributors, this was beneficial to each party involved. I have since contributed 100s of online articles to these type sites and I continue to receive revenue share payments from them to date.

8

I have not gotten wealthy from this venue but it has at times been a nice supplement to my income. I personally have had more success with book and e-book sales; however the contributions I made to content websites, actually trained me toward much better writing and editing skills that I was later able to incorporate into my books (more on book and e-book publishing in <u>CHAPTER FIVE</u>).

I did also have negative experiences with particular content websites. In one case of my canceling my membership with a site, I had contributed approximately 80 articles to a "How-To" type property that shared Adsense revenue with authors who wrote for them.

The payments grew to a very nice level and I was being paid from my Google Adsense Account, which was deposited into my bank account, on a fairly regular basis.

In order for Google to release Adsense payments, they must reach a $100.00 threshold and mine began reaching this about every other month and so I was obviously pleased and excited.

At one point I noticed that my revenue began to accumulate much more slowly and I immediately knew something had changed with one of the sites I was writing for. In my Adsense account, which allows you to create "channels", meaning individualized viewing of how much revenue each site you contribute-to is generating, I noticed that this 'How-To' site's revenue dropped completely off. It was showing zero revenue week after week, following a period of time when revenue was showing up almost daily.

I contacted the site by email, asking why I was no longer receiving Adsense Revenue shares from my content on their site and they explained that they discontinued sharing the site's revenue with contributors. I asked why they did not inform me of this and they stated that they had sent out a blanket email to all contributors explaining this. I not only did not receive the email but other fellow-writers, whom I knew outside of the site but who also wrote for them also did not receive the notification email. We were able to ascertain that the delay in contributors receiving notifications was so-that the site could continue to glean from them as many more pieces of content as possible.

They would do this before some of the members could cancel their memberships in response to the unfair change.

The site further informed me that their contributor agreement specifies that they could make these type changes "at any time, without notice" but that contributors would be informed and given opportunity to discontinue their contributions should they so decide. I responded by asking the site to remove all of my content from their pages and that if they did not do so, I would be seeking legal action against them and they agreed to do so. I was actually surprised that they did not invite me to take any action I wished and that they would respond with their own legal action but thankfully it did not come to that.

A similar negative experience I had with a content website, sharing revenue with members, involved them not accruing my page-views in my account. The counter remained at zero for an extended period of time after I began publishing dozens of content-pieces. Upon my inquiring with them about it, they pointed out that I failed to complete a particular item of registration, if I remember correctly, having to do with my tax information.

It would have seemed logical for them to have let the page-view counter run in the mean time but this was one of many methods they used to hold back contributor revenue. I supplied the needed information and continued to contribute to the website.

I then experienced a point at which my accumulated revenue, which was only a few dollars, was suddenly rolled back to zero. I again inquired as to why this had occurred and this time, they pointed out that I had not properly selected a prompt on a recent piece of content I published (having to do with categories if I remember correctly) and that the rolled-back revenue was a penalty for this. I saw where other contributors were complaining on other website forums about this content site, saying that they were not being paid for their articles due to being outside of the USA but that they were unaware of this policy (it was stated in their agreement but somewhat vaguely). You would think that when they submitted all of their information to be paid revenue shares, someone with the site administration would have then emailed them explaining this.

Instead, the site did not want to risk not gleaning content from these members and so they remained somewhat elusive regarding the issue.

I ended up canceling my membership with this content site as well but because of about 75 pieces of my content being placed by me, in a particular revenue share category when I published them, they refused to remove them from their site. Almost four years later (all the while, the site earning revenue on my content), I found information stating that the site had changed administration and so I asked them if I could rejoin them as a contributor (the new management sounded promising). They agreed and reopened my account and I began to submit content to them, which reached about 130 new pieces I published on the site.

I also submitted five articles to them under a more exclusive revenue share category and upon reviewing them, an editor informed me that I was no longer a member and he referred to my earlier self-cancellation with the site, from over three years previously. He stated that I could ask that my account be reopened and afterward I could resubmit the exclusive articles (I had already done so and was accepted).

I responded by canceling my membership once-again, this-time permanently because my account had not only **already been reinstated** but I was publishing and submitting new articles with them, which would have been impossible to do without current membership. This was a bad sign in my opinion and I felt I could not trust the site to properly accrue any payments due to me or that if they did begin well with me, they might find a bogus reason at a later date to discontinue my membership or to roll-back my revenue.

I was not willing to degrade my authored work again, on their site, as had occurred in the past. While I hope this will not come across offensive I feel this type of relationship with a content site, in-essence is requiring authors to prostitute their work. This is a term I once heard a fellow-author use on a publishing forum, when referring to some venues writers will accept that degrades their authorship and while it is a blunt statement to use regarding this type issue, I feel it is a legitimate analogy.

Are all content sites involved in the bogus or dishonest type practices, such as those I have described above?

Certainly not, in-fact there are many highly-ethical and reputable websites that provide benefit and reasonable respect to contributors as I stated in my introduction. I am very pleased with one content site in-particular that I have written for, who has been faithful to compute and pay me monthly for page-views that accrue on my content that appears on their pages. I was also impressed with their promptness to communicate with writers and to respond to any problems on the site as they occurred.

I did have issue with one particular editor on the site, who required changes on some of my articles that actually changed the theme and meaning of them however, there were other editors who were very reasonable with their required changes on my submitted content. I do not feel this editor was intentionally trying to enforce her own style onto my articles but rather felt she was doing me a service. Her required changes did however result in exactly that – a change in the original meanings of sections in my articles.

I reported this issue to the administration who defended the actions of the editor and so I respectfully discontinued writing for the site.

I actually could have stayed on with them and written for other topics on the site as I had in the past and having had no serious problems with the editors over those. I felt however that this particular issue was serious enough, that my resigning would possibly help the administration to take the issue of overboard editing requirements more seriously, for the sake of future writers submitting content to that particular topic.

It is not possible to find a site to submit articles or other works of content to, that will be perfect in every respect. It's also possible that I set my own standards for sites I chose to write for, a little too high but some of this came from my previous negative experiences with sites that had serious issues that were not being resolved. It might also help a content producer, looking for a site to join, to conduct an online search, using the site(s) name(s) in a search engine, to see if there are positive or negative reviews of them being posted. There are actually websites and blogs whose sole purpose is reviewing websites and providing information regarding their revenue earnings and net worth.

These can provide valuable information when considering websites for participation in.

In the Chapters that follow, I will point out other basic things one should look for, when deciding what type of site(s) they choose to submit their articles and content works to.

CHAPTER TWO

Things to Consider in a Content Revenue Site Contract

Is the agreement a site offers to become a content producer, overly one-sided in their benefit?

While a website certainly has to protect itself when offering content producer agreements, they should also demonstrate that they are interested in helping their members succeed as well. The contracted members are after-all the very life-blood of their website and without them, they also would not succeed. It is typical for example for content sites to warn of canceling memberships, should a content producer plagiarize on their site (stealing content from other sources and republishing it is their own). It is also typical for them to ask members not to spam their site under warning of canceled membership. This would include things such as redirecting links in articles (ones that take readers to other sites for marketing purposes); adding more links than are allowed, within the body of an article and when content producers overly promote themselves in articles.

18

They also have a right to warn members not to extract their software (illegal hacking), such as parts of their publishing platform, to use on their own sites, or to sell to others. Lastly, they have a right to restrict the use of profanity, bigotry of any kind and obscenity in any form.

What might send up a red flag however in regard to a contributor agreement, are things such as warnings that a member's account can be canceled "at any time and for any reason" or that the site's policies can be changed "at anytime without notice". It would be better for an agreement to state that members can lose membership for legitimate reasons specified and that any changes in the agreement will be updated with a 15 or 30 day notice to contributors. Not having these type terms, does not necessarily mean that a site is not a good venue for a content producer but all of these type things should be evaluated and considered together as a whole when choosing a site to contribute content to.

Another very important consideration is whether or not a content site allows members to retain the copyrights to their submitted content or if it becomes the perpetual, exclusive property of the site.

In some cases, sites require totally original content that has not been published elsewhere, on any other online or in-print source previously. This-too is not necessarily a bad thing and possibly even a positive, as long as the contributor can remove the content or have it removed, in the event they resign with the website or have their membership canceled at some point.

Does the content producer agreement warn of penalties that may occur, even if common or honest mistakes are made by members?

Breaking policies like those I have described in the previous subheading are legitimate reasons for a content producer's membership at a site to be canceled. If however the reasons for losing membership listed include things such as not having logged-in to one's account for 30, 60 or even 90 days, not contributing a certain number of content-pieces within a set amount of time (unless reasonable and achievable) or having improperly categorized an article, these are unreasonably strict policies in my opinion and a strong reason to reconsider joining a site who enforces them.

I mention this because some circumstances are beyond one's control, such as an illness that keeps one from going online for months at a time or a new content producer who inadvertently uses a prompt on a publishing platform incorrectly, as they are learning better publishing skills.

If however the site is one that pays high-level compensation or base salaries, these type requirements are then reasonably required and understandably needed.

To offer an example of a policy a site enforced in their agreement that required me to inquire with them after I published content on their site, had to do with "members clicking on their own articles" (the site paid contributors per page views). Their agreement stated that generating clicks on articles that were not legitimate views by site visitors would result in the immediate and permanent cancellation of a contributor's membership (false clicks). At the same time, the site encouraged contributors to link to other articles on the site they had written (allowing three links on new articles).

I found that linking to my other articles on the site required me to go to my articles-list on the site and to click on those I wanted to link-to, in order to copy and paste the links into new articles.

I wrote to the site administration, to make sure that by my doing this, I was not endangering my membership with the site but I did not receive a response on the inquiry. My suspicion however, is that they would have told me that clicking on one's own links on the site for this purpose was permissible, since it was actually a benefit to them, in helping to increase traffic to other articles on the site. I did wonder however if this scenario had occurred to them and that it might have been a detail that could have been added to that particular term in their content producer agreement. This same type scenario would also apply to authors who copy/paste their article-links at forums or social networks they frequented, to promote their works.

Certainly an author can copy/paste all of their article links on one page and save them as a document-file to avoid unnecessary clicks on their content.

The forethought for doing this type thing however, is not always there when authors are inexperienced or are not offered instruction for doing this, to avoid false click suspicions. This demonstrates that content producer contract terms, are not always as "cut and dried" (as easily adhered-to) as sites would like them to be and that if a contracted member feels they are being unduly reprimanded or wrongly ejected from membership for a violation, they should be given opportunity to offer explanation for their questionable actions. I mention this because in worse-case scenarios dishonest websites have actually resorted to bogus excuses for canceling memberships, in order to retain a contributor's content or to avoid having to pay-out revenue shares due to them.

Does the site have a responsive administration, willing to communicate to the needs, problems or questions of content producers?

Nothing can be more frustrating to a content site member who cannot get the administration to respond to them.

Issues that can arise may include things such as seeing content suddenly disappear from one's account, accrued revenue payments not being received or experiencing bugs in the publishing software that prevents new content from being submitted properly.

The site should take interest in these type issues because members who can stay active in contributing content, without these type hindrances, will continue to increase the site's traffic and revenue.

Some content sites are very large and understandably, these types can find difficulty in responding individually to massive numbers of emails.

Many remedy this problem by providing a "Questions & Answers" page on their site and/or by providing a contributor's forum, where problems and issues can be discussed with members who have already experienced them and can recommend solutions to newer members (more regarding forums under the next sub-heading).

Is the site lacking good screening of improper content being published on the site?

Another important step a content producer should take is to browse the pages of websites they are considering membership with. Is it reader-friendly? Is the site-layout easy to navigate? Do they allow offensive material on the site? Does their publishing software offer "word check" (spelling and punctuation corrections)? These type questions have to do with a site's quality and are very important considerations. I personally for example, canceled membership at a content website, due to the increased allowing of religious bigotry and offensive article posts that were commonly being added to their pages by contributors. Many contained material that was close to pornographic and as the site-administration continued to fail in removing this type content, it began to increase and site was no longer reader-friendly overall.

The site obviously wanted to see the most content possible on their pages but increased revenue, versus an eventually degraded reputation for a website, is not a good trade in my opinion.

Of course this is a different story if a site actually rallies in this type of content but in this case, a content producer will be able to recognize this fact and add it into their considerations in deciding whether or not to join the site.

The same is true of content site forums that degrade over time due to lack of moderation. Are forum members attacking each other on the forum? Are offensive posts in-general being allowed? These are important questions as well because the intent of content site forums should be to exchange needed or interesting information, while respect for fellow-members is also being demonstrated. The forum should reflect the same quality and theme as the site in-general displays in the content they allow to be published.

CHAPTER THREE

Getting your own Blog or Website to Generate Revenue

Another method for publishing content and adding monetization to it via Google Adsense or through other paid advertising venues is to be set up with a personal blog or website. While it's true that starting from scratch with a new site can take time to promote and to gain substantial traffic (visitors), it does have its advantages.

One advantage is that you are in-control as the site administrator and you can choose the template for it (general design and theme) and you can design the overall layout of the site, to your liking.

You may also choose to add a forum to the site if your hosting company (provider of your website publishing tools) provides this option or allows readers to post comments beneath the articles you publish on it.

Another advantage is that you can own the domain of your website or blog (the registered online address of it).

This makes the site's name and online address uniquely yours and prevents anyone else from registering the same domain that you become owner of (may need to be renewed yearly). This would also give you the liberty to provide readers visiting your site, with the type of content you decide to publish on it, whether it's one subject or multiple ones.

In the case of a blog, some site-owners actually publish stories about their selves and other information with a more personal type touch to it and others actually make their blogs into life-journals that document interesting occurrences in their lives (i.e. a medical condition, their travels, recipes they enjoy, etc…).

There are many website and blog hosting companies online to choose from. Many have affordable cost-effective rates and others actually offer free hosting. I personally have a "blogger" site (a blog hosted by the Google Company) and my domain registration (optional) is only $10.00 per year. I have incorporated Google Adsense into the site and readers can post comments on my articles, which I can personally moderate or delete as needed (i.e. spam posts or offensive ones).

I do however feel it is important to determine the needs of your site, such as how many megabits and how much bandwidth a host offers through their websites and how many pages you can add to your site (many offer unlimited space and pages).

The convenience of a blog is also in the fact that these will automatically archive each post you make, by month, day and year, so that as you post each new article, this is done for you. When seeking options on blogs or websites through hosting companies, doing an online search to read what is offered on these and comparing the costs of them can help one determine which type site would work best for them.

CHAPTER FOUR

My Plagiarism and Article Re-publishing Observations

(When Online Content is Stolen)

I recently posted the information following below, on an online forum that was not available to the public. The post was in regard to the subject of "plagiarism" (theft of intellectual property) and I feel the things I shared are worthy of being included as a chapter in this book.

My Post:

"When I was an editor for a thyroid health website, where I published 163 articles, I underwent training which included an extensive course on plagiarism. I wanted to share some thoughts on the subject that came from that course I took and from other sources I've learned facts on the subject from, over the past 8 years I've been publishing online.

First I want to express that I'm absolutely against plagiarism which amounts to theft of intellectual property.

At the same time, I've had experiences that made me realize the importance in being absolutely sure something I've published online has been plagiarized by someone else before making that accusation toward them.

One experience I had in this area was when after publishing two articles on the subject of thyroid cancer, for the thyroid health site previously mentioned, another editor for another topic on the site wrote a very similar set of two articles that had similar titles and similar outlines to mine. I was quite upset until closer reading of the articles and I realized they had more originality in them than I first recognized and the timing of their articles following mine only weeks later and the other basic similarities to mine was simply a fluke.

Even if this was not the case and their idea for these was sparked by my articles it still did not meet the definition of plagiarism. The experience made me re-examine myself for the possibility that I actually felt the other editor presented me some competition and that was actually where part of my concern was coming from.

My point being that if you feel you've been plagiarized, it is important to be specific if you plan to point it out to a party suspected of the plagiarism or others you may wish to involve in getting the issue resolved.

I've also previously wrote 70-plus articles for a "how-to" content site and have seen my outlines for these followed very closely by other how-to online properties. As far as republishing my own articles after having them on other sites, I have only done so from ones that allowed this and when I felt a need to do so as backup because some sites will not necessarily be around months or years from now.

I have also republished articles at times because sites I resigned from began a process of over-writing them when I left (replacing them, rather than deleting them) and a new editor would be stepping in. This occurred at the thyroid health site I describe above for example. I in-fact moved most of my thyroid subject articles over to my personal blog from that site for this reason and not solely for Adsense revenue purposes because republishing articles on more than one site can drop your Google rating as an author.

I have over 600 articles online to date, with only about 100 of them being republished from the thyroid health site.

I hope I'm never accused of plagiarism myself because for me personally, that would be somewhat of a slap in the face. I began search and research on health disorders (mostly the ones I am experiencing) in 2003 and have put more study hours behind this than some medical students have, who have become doctors (literally). I first began creating a website called "JimLow's Articles & Audios", in late 2004, where I published about 125 articles on thyroid, CFS, adrenal fatigue, anxiety, MVP, etc... I also moved those articles at one point upon canceling the site because I did not want to continue paying a hosting fee, when free hosting was available.

I did not place Google Adsense on that original site for two years because my purpose was writing and sharing knowledge with fellow health disorder patients and not to make money from the articles. I am now making revenue every way possible from my content because I realized over time, this does not diminish the benefit to readers of the articles and is a nice little benefit for me, the author and for the advertisers as well.

It would take a lot more time and effort for me to plagiarize than to write an article from scratch, drawing from my own knowledge. Do I write on subjects that have already been covered? Absolutely and so does everyone else with exception of the very first writers who originally covered subjects decades or 100s of years ago. Same subjects are covered endlessly online and if they weren't, we would have a very empty-looking internet.

Site administrations on most content sites have a feature in their software that searches for duplicate content before they accept submissions. If at some point, you feel your content has been stolen you can point-out your concern to them and ask them if they can run a duplicate content check for you. The same thing can be done by pasting content from an article (titles and whole sentences) into a Google search, to see if it has been published by anyone else or use free online programs such as the Copyscape Plagiarism Checker."

Sites who Use Content without Permission

I have also experienced times of needing to ask sites who posted my content without my permission, to remove it. This is not the same as plagiarism in which an article-publisher claims to have written a piece that they actually extracted in-part or in-full from someone else's authored content. In this case it would actually come under "copyright infringement" and "intellectual property theft" definitions. One site I recently contacted for committing this offense by publishing my content in-full on their site without permission was in regard to an article I wrote on the subject of "invention marketing". The owners of the website were in this line of work their selves (consultation for inventors) and I found on one of their pages, where they had pasted my article-content. I wrote to them via their online contact form and asked them to remove it immediately. They were gracious and responded immediately and offered to instead, simply mention the article and post a link to it, which I accepted as resolution to the issue.

This still gave them some benefit and for me as well, by helping to promote my article at the original link-source.

It is usually acceptable to quote small portions of content from another source, as long at it is only a snippet that's about 25 words in length and up to a maximum of 50 words. The author or source should be credited by name for the original article the quote is extracted from and a link to the content should be added. Most authors have no problem with someone quoting them, under these conditions and at the same time, the source quoting them is showing respect for their intellectual property.

CHAPTER FIVE

Tips on other Types of Publishing and Republishing

Formatting Books and E-books from Articles

Some content producers eventually compile articles they have written, into books and e-books. This can be done, as long as any articles one has published on content sites are not exclusive to them (all re-publishing rights turned over to them).

Some content sites ask only for an exclusive on "digital rights" meaning anything online or downloadable on electronic reading devices, such as e-books belongs to them. In this case an in-print book can still be published by the original author of them.

Other content sites ask for an exclusive on articles for only a set amount of time, such as one year and afterward, the author can republish them, any way they wish.

Following, are tips on how to format articles into a format that can be published as a book or e-book:

One important early step is to look at other e-books and in-print books by reputable authors or publishers and use them as a guideline as far as book-structure goes. You'll note that a lot of them have the title and subtitle on the first page and possibly the author credit and copyright notation on the first page as well.

You'll notice that their next page might have a "dedication" (optional depending on type of book but can be added to any book) and in most cases is short – sometimes even just a sentence in length.

Afterward, a page for the "Table of Contents" listing chapter-titles can be added and then a page that gives an "Introduction" to your book (some books place table of contents after the intro and vice-versa). Each article you place in the book can serve as a chapter.

The next page after the Table of Contents can start "CHAPTER ONE" with the chapter's title in bold, in all large caps or underlined (different authors may do one or a combination of these).

The content of the chapter would then be in regular print (no bold or all large caps words unless for highlighting).

With each new chapter/article, you simply do the same as I describe in the previous paragraph and at the end of the book you can add a "Conclusion" if you like but that-too is optional and depends on the type of book being published.

As far as indenting paragraphs, I use the double-space method, rather than indenting because I wrote for two very large content sites and their studies of site-visitors showed in regard to indentations versus double-spacing, that readers prefer double space paragraph separations (again other authors or publishers may disagree with using this method in books).

Also know that when you submit an e-book to most publishing platforms, they allow you to preview the file as it would look to a NOOK, Kindle or other e-book reader before you complete the publishing of it. If you see things not right in your word file, simply "save" your book submission information and don't publish until you've updated your file the way you want it to look.

Afterward, you can reload the book's content (word file) into the book file prompt when it is revised to your liking.

As far as page-numbering, Word.Doc files can be numbered – just look for the "Insert" prompt at the top of your word processor screen and select the type page numbering and at what page you want numbering to begin. What's nice about Microsoft Word page numbering is that the numbering will also appear if you convert your file to PDF (free conversion is offered online, via a Yahoo search).

This last part of advice will be more-so the advice some publishers may differ with me on but I have all of my own titles published on several large booksellers without professional editing applied to them. YES, pro-editing would improve them even more but with my having about 39 e-book titles and nearly as many books-in-print, it would be a massive expense for me to have this done in any way other than gradually, over time. In the mean-time, I wanted my information available out there, so published them at very near professionally edited level.

There are problems you'll have to deal with, including the fact that Word files will change to a different layout, when you covert them to PDF or EPUB but not always so significantly that it seriously affects the quality of your book. Some publishers (fee-based ones) will try to convince you that publishing from Word.Doc files; even with conversions is a big no-no! – But, this is what I have done with all my books and I get great comments on them often from readers. In my case, with health-related titles, rather than novels, people are far more interested in my info, than in the professionally-detailed layout of my titles.

In-short, if you're publishing a novel, professional editing may be important but if your book is need-to-know information (i.e. How-To, Self-Education, etc…) a professional editor may be an expense that is not necessarily needed. I would however, run the content-file through word/grammar check and proof-reading of it to a willing listener/reader to make sure it flows as you would like.

Recording Audios for Publishing on Websites

Audios were something I enjoyed producing, for placing on content sites because I have personally always enjoyed informative information and books I could listen to via Mp3 downloads or on tape and CD. I did find however, that audios do not receive as many clicks as do written works, so keep this in mind if you decide to submit audio content to revenue sharing websites.

There are software downloads available that allow you to simply plug your own audio player, into the back of your computer sound board and record audios that convert into Mp3 files that you can post on websites that are set up to accept them as content for use by site-visitors. What you need to accomplish this, is a player with an earphone jack (one that plays-back audio tapes and/or CDs) and a wire you can buy at a Radio Shack or other electronics stores with the standard-size male-jack on each end (the type seen on the end of earphones). You simply plug one end into the earphone input and the other into the "blue" input on the back of your computer tower's sound board.

This blue input should be right next to the green input, where your computer speakers are plugged in.

The audio you play through the wire from the player, into the computer will have already been pre-recorded using a microphone, containing the audio you wish to make into an Mp3 file. The computer recording software should allow you to hear what you are playing-recording, through your computer speakers. It should also have adjustable recording levels you click on to adjust, a choice of mono or stereo and other effects that might be needed. In fact you can also adjust the volume, by simply doing so from the player you are using.

Some of the audios I've posted on content websites are better than others. The reason for this is because it took me a while to find the better audio recording programs online and to know how to adjust the recording levels and other adjustments to make best-possible recordings. In reality, these different software providers make these programs easy to use and I should have experimented a bit more before posting as many audio downloads as I did so quickly on content sites.

When I say "experiment", once you record a file, your own computer saves it in a file and you can click and play it back on your own media-player, to see how it sounds before publishing it.

To obtain software for downloading and recording audios, simply conduct a search on Google and use the search term "record tapes to CDs". Following are the names of some I've used that can also be found via online search: "Blaze Audio", "Golden Records" and "Polderbits". When you find any of these, choose their "free download" option because this allows a free trial of them for about two weeks before you purchase the permanent versions.

I have always loved audios and they are wonderful method for sharing interesting information, stories, music and knowledge.

Some websites also allow video content to be posted by contributors, including that they have personally created or that they link-to from sources that feature videos and who allow links to them (i.e. YouTube). Some sites also allow images to be posted as content by those who have rights to them.

This would include contributors who practice photography and have interesting images to offer for view by site-visitors. All of these types of content have potential to create page-views and/or clicks on ads provided to content sites by advertising firms.

In Conclusion of SECTION ONE:

It is my hope that the preceding chapters have offered sound advice to content producers who are seeking to benefit from websites who offer revenue opportunities. I would only add in closing that one should take the time to research the sites they are considering and to not make snap-decisions in choosing those for submitting content to. This demonstrates that one places real value on their intellectual works, plus it is simply good business to look out for one's own interest when entering into business relationships, online and otherwise.

SECTION TWO

How To Avoid Negative Online Publishing Experiences

Cautiously Marketing Your Intellectual Property

TABLE OF CONTENTS (SECTION TWO):

INTRODUCTION:

Approximately 7% of all retail sales occur online presently and business research firms predict that up to 210-billion dollars in total sales will be accomplished online for the year 2011 with an estimated 8% of total retail sales being predicted for 2012 or up to 250-billion dollars worth. Much of this business is in the area of published works, such as books and e-books being sold by reputable publishers including Amazon and Barnes & Noble and by reputable content websites that offer free public articles but who generate massive advertising income and retail sales (i.e. Associated Content Yahoo and About.com). Strangely enough, even with this type of growth in online business, there are still companies, large and small, and individuals who conduct electronic commerce, with a seeming lack of seriousness in regard to business ethics but with profit earnings as a high priority at the same time. It is almost as if they perceive long distance transactions as being something one does not have to conduct with the same ethics or moral standards as one would practice with interstate commerce that is conducted in-person or that requires some type of physical exchange.

48

In worse case scenarios, online businesses actually trifle with people or slight them and some actually cheat their customers or clients, as a regular practice. It's possible that they feel at more liberty to do so because of the fact that it is difficult at this point in time, to prosecute for illegal online transactions that occur or to even register complaints against some online businesses, who do not reveal their physical locations and who provide only a contact phone number but who reveal very little about their companies otherwise. While all computers have a unique IP address (Internet Protocol) and can be tracked by this and located by authorized legal officials, individual citizens cannot do so because such a practice can be considered illegal, when it is not authorized. Even large companies who do openly display their contact information can be difficult to investigate for dishonest online transactions, due to the fact that their electronic records can be manipulated and difficult to track.

There are ways however, that we as individuals who purchase from online business or who become involved with them in other ways (i.e. authoring content for publishers or websites) can call bad online business practices into question, when we are affected by them.

This can be done legally but with effective results. If we, who care about the future of electronic commerce, can begin to exercise our rights to be dealt-with honestly by online businesses, it can help to influence them, in a positive future direction.

If we fail to do our part however, the internet, over time will begin to progressively cheapen in the area of content publishing and it will begin to become increasingly difficult to protect against unethical activity. This has already begun to occur on a wide scale but with some effort, we can begin to reverse this downward trend, while it is still possible to do so.

Within the chapters that follow, I will offer suggestions for helping to remedy experiences one might have with dishonest online entities or ones who fail to see reasonable interests required by those who enter into business arrangements with them and how to also avoid such experiences.

I will cite several personal examples of questionable activities, practiced by online businesses I have dealt with, that negatively affected me, in the area of online publishing.

Certainly these same type practices occur in the area of retail sales as well and likely on an even larger scale but I feel my experiences, as well as my advice may help to provide ideas of how one can take a proactive stance in helping to effect positive change in electronic commerce of every type, including that which is conducted in the written content publishing field -- the marketing of intellectual property.

CHAPTER ONE

Avoiding Fly-By-Night Online Businesses

(A Simple Rule of Thumb)

As mentioned in the introduction of this book, there are online businesses, who reveal as little about their companies as possible. They may not have an "About Us" page at all or if they do include one on their website, it contains very little information about them. The more up-front type websites include lots of information about their companies, including a list of their founders and/or CEOs, the type of experience their staff has in regard to the business they are conducting and information about their office location (i.e. their physical address, phone number and email or fax lists).

When these type things are not included, this should raise a red flag to people who are browsing certain types of businesses online. Even when companies are new, one should feel far more comfortable dealing with them, if they reveal important information regarding their background and business operations.

This, as opposed to them seemingly being elusive with this type of information. In some cases, unethical businesses avoid posting details about their companies because they want to be able to shut down their operations if needed, should they be pursued legally and leave very little trail behind them for being tracked down by authorities or investigating bureaus.

These type companies are referred to as "fly-by-night" businesses, a term that has been around for a very long time and they certainly do exist online, although some may operate for many years before shutting down and reorganizing.

In regard to publishing companies for example, I looked into some of these for publishing my books and e-books, that were far less reputable than are the well-established ones but after careful investigation via online search, I decided that it would be a mistake to go with any of them.

Much of my decision was also based on the fact that some of these publishers were fee-based print-on-demand (POD) companies.

With the fact that even mainstream publishers, such as Amazon and Barnes & Noble, can publish e-books and books in-print on a POD basis, at no cost to the author/publisher, it would have been fallacy for me to have gone with these other publishers, on my low budget.

In addition to suggesting that one beware of online businesses that reveal little about their companies on their websites, I would also advise that it would be a good idea to conduct an online search of companies you are considering entering into business with, to see what their past clients are saying about them. This can be done simply by placing their name in the bar of a search engine. If a company has been in operation for any reasonable length of time, information will be found that is either positive or negative and possibly some of both, in which case one must balance the information found, best possible. While these suggestions may seem simple, they fall in line with the old saying, that "you can't judge a book by its cover". There are flashy, very technical looking websites that exist online, who are totally lacking in any proper business ethics and good business practices and one would do well to remember this fact.

CHAPTER TWO

The Better Business Bureau: Not Just a Slap on the Wrist

(Bringing Resolution to Bad Online Business Practices)

It is sometimes believed that turning a company or an individual conducting bad business, over to the Better Business Bureau (BBB) for mediation of a complaint, is ineffective and amounts to no more than simply a "slap on the wrist". This is not true however because unless they resolve complaints that are registered against them or they at least attempt to resolve them, they will remain on their BBB record as "UNRESOLVED" for three years. Many potential customers of businesses will look up their BBB complaint record, before doing business with them and this can be quickly accomplished online. If they find a large number of complaints or they see one or more complaints that have not been resolved within a reasonable period of time of them being registered, this is enough deterrent for many customers or clients to refrain from doing business with them.

BBB records can also be instrumental toward establishing the ongoing reputation of businesses.

In my approximate 8 years of dealing with publishing businesses, online, I have only had to resort to BBB complaints against two. The companies did however resolve these complaints quickly; one doing so within 48 hours and the other doing so within a week of my registering a complaint. It should be understood that some businesses who are BBB accredited, meaning they have membership with this mediating bureau, are sometimes given good ratings by the BBB, due to their promptness in attempting to resolve complaints registered against them. This is what the rating system is based on and it is not a rating of a company's business ethics in-general. Most people who do background checks on businesses, at the BBB website, are aware of this fact and so they also take into consideration, the number of complaints a company has against it and the nature of those complaints (i.e. contractual complaints or sales complaints, etc…). Also, if a business is BBB accredited, they are required to resolve complaints registered against them, within 30 days.

If a complaint is not initially resolved, they are then required to enter into mediation/arbitration with the complainer, to further attempt a resolution. The resulting status of "resolved" or "unresolved" is then, afterward displayed on their record for approximately 36 months.

The BBB has made it simple to fill out their online complaint form and by doing so; this places the complaint into the hands of the business in question, very quickly. Regardless of where a business may be located within the United States, a person complaining can register a complaint from the BBB office within their own state, since this would be the location from which they conducted their side of the business transaction resulting in a legitimately negative experience for them.

Businesses who are attempting to build an honest and ethical reputation, do not like seeing numerous complaints or unresolved complaints displayed publicly on their BBB record. For this reason, it can be an effective move on the part of a consumer or business associate, to register a BBB complaint when on the receiving end of dishonest or unethical business practices by online companies.

Certainly, if one has been cheated out of thousands of dollars or their intellectual property has been stolen from them, legal representation, involving an actual lawsuit should be pursued but for milder but concerning offenses, the BBB is often an effective choice of remedy.

CHAPTER THREE

My Heated Exchange with an Online Beatles Radio Station

(Putting the Blue Meanies in Their Proper Place)

I had a recent experience with getting into a tiff with a man who runs an online Beatles radio station website (I'm a lifetime fan of the rock group) and the fact that our correspondence evolved into a nasty exchange took me a bit by surprise. My problem involved my having sent them a PDF file of a book I had written, in consideration of being sold in their online store, which was a follow-up to my earlier email, asking if they were interested in reviewing the book, which they replied to in the affirmative. I simply requested conformation of their receipt of my intellectual property, within the submission I sent, which I had to request two additional times over a two month period because they would not respond. This was somewhat of a red flag to me because I had some authored works that were in-essence stolen from me previous to this.

The previous incident was under very similar circumstances but I was fortunately able to resolve by complaint through the Better Business Bureau.

When the station owner did finally respond, he referred to my authored Beatles book titled *A Fan's Tribute to the Beatles* as "crap", in spite of not having read it and he called me a few choice names via email and ones that would actually fall under internet harassment laws in the US (his business is located in the UK). He resorted to this because he felt I had given his wife, who runs the radio station's corresponding Beatles memorabilia store a "difficult time" in my complaining about not receiving confirmation from them of receiving my book files by email attachment. He also said he was going to write a negative review for my book, place it online and send me a link to it once completed (Oh how vile thou art revenge!).

I had no idea the man would respond in this fashion simply because I expressed my disappointment in regard to his dropped communications with me, after I sent further information and PDF/Word files of the aforementioned book to him.

This was for consideration of distribution for it, through his online store (at his request). I specifically asked that he please confirm receipt of the files and information I submitted to him because this gives me documentation when I send my authored material to someone via e-mail, especially to overseas locations. I also had to reformat the book because it had been converted into EPUB at one point for publication on the Google E-book Store and this was the only version I had saved (I now save both PDF and Word files of all of my books for backup). I had to re-separate all of the headings, re-do paragraph separations etc... for sending to the Beatles store and it took me most of a full day to do so.

I had no idea who ran the Beatles memorabilia store (this information was not included on their website), which was an extension of the radio station, in-fact I suspected it was pretty much a one man operation and that both the radio station and store were a one-man show (this was not far from correct). By no means was I purposefully intending to direct anything derogatory toward this man's wife, as was his accusation (she became the contact regarding my book submission to them).

He was the person I was in contact with originally and I had no idea his wife even existed! I suspected that the lady, who responded to my email regarding their lack of confirmation for receipt of my copyrighted materials, was either an employee of the radio station or someone using an online nickname (she signed her response with a first-name only). The station-owner uses a nickname, derived from the title of a Beatle's song, rather than his real name and this is partly why I felt this woman was doing this as well. While I've listened to the radio station myself a number of times over the past few years, I had never once heard her name mentioned or the fact that the website owner even had a wife.

This entire episode started with my sending the PDF and Word files of my Beatle title book, which is a "fan's tribute", not a biography or a novel but simply a personal view of my love for Beatles music and my admiration for the men who wrote such beautiful songs. It is a short-length book (about 50 pages – no images). I do make mention of life-struggles these men have experienced as well as some Christian views I added-in.

This included my mention that John Lennon repeatedly apologized for his remarks regarding the popularity of the Beatles as compared to that of Jesus Christ, which he made in the year 1966. I also mention John's period of seeking information on the Christian faith, including letters he wrote to Oral Roberts Ministries and donations he made to them at one time. My intention was to create a book that wasn't a typical "cutesie Beatles mop tops" repeat, with so many of these already being offered by booksellers. I actually wondered if something included in the book was offensive to the owners of the radio station but it turns out that their failure to confirm receipt of my submission was simply neglect on their part. With the fact that my intellectual property was involved, I simply had to follow through to protect my interests and their silence was logically very concerning to me.

When I originally wrote the man at the Beatles radio station asking if he might be interested in adding either the e-book or the in-print version to their online store product line, he replied within about two days. He stated in his email, requesting further information that the e-book version might be a good prospect for the store, with their recent adding of digital downloads to the site.

I responded in telling him I would send PDF and Word files to him for review as mentioned previously. Once a full month had past I asked once again, via a new email for confirmation that he received my files, but still no answer. Once yet another full month passed I sent an email expressing my disappointment that he didn't confirm my submission and that even a polite "no" answer would have sufficed, which obviously came across very offensive to him (my e-mail did not venture outside of professional etiquette).

His wife responded first to the email but I had no idea who she was and I actually suspected it to be the site owner pulling a prank, due to numerous misspellings and a lack of professionalism the response contained. My short response to them, that followed, should not have come across offensive but apparently it did (my request was good business and common protocol). I hold no animosity for this online Beatles radio station or toward the couple who run it however, when he informed me that a bad review of what he called my "crap book" was on its way to being posted online, I wanted to have my own rebuttal handy as well.

The response I wrote might be more properly categorized as "my side of the story", that I also planned to publish online if necessary. He did not follow through with the vengeful, negative review and so I was not required to rebut any negative press from him either.

This is not actually the first time I have seen online correspondence turn sour, in-fact, some of the worst mud-slinging I have witnessed in my lifetime was on forums, message boards and even within article exchanges between authors at odds with each other. In my opinion, some of this is a form of venting anger and frustrations one has, toward those who are not actually responsible for their problems but that is being masked as anger toward the individuals it may be directed at. I personally try to avoid it, when I see hints of it being directed toward me by someone and in most cases when a person has sloughed me off, after I have gone to some effort to follow through on a mutually considered business prospect I simply walk away. In hindsight, that's what I wish I had done in this case involving the online Beatle radio station and despite the tiff that developed between us, I only wish them growing and ongoing success (sincerely).

At the same time, it was my obligation to point out their lack of proper business protocol and hopefully, it will make them think twice before slighting someone else, who is following-through on a business proposal, that they-themselves have requested to be submitted to them.

The fact that business is being conducted online, rather than in-person, should not change its priority or the proper ethics with which it is conducted, especially with the fact that more companies, banks and other business institutions are now conducting transactions online, than at any previous time in our history and this trend continues to increase with each passing day. We, who are at the forefront of this growth, should determine to set a high standard of precedence for the future of online business and electronic commerce.

CHAPTER FOUR

Removing my Blog from a Major Revenue Sharing Website Conglomerate

(The Strange Practices of a High-Profile Content Farm)

I wish to mention at the beginning of this chapter, that the business practices of the website I will be mentioning following, are not in the "corrupt" or "dishonest" categories, nor are they necessarily unethical; they do however represent an over-emphasis of benefit for the website with an imbalanced lack of consideration for writers who contract with them, in my opinion (many former writers for them, share my view, while others view them very positively).

One reason I decided to write an article/chapter, actually naming a revenue-sharing content website is due to seeing many other writers specifically give their evaluations/revues of their experiences with Demand Studios, and so I thought I would add my own into the mix, for balance.

67

Certainly this will not be an attack toward them however, I will be expressing some disagreement with their methods, all of which they consider to be under their editing and quality-of-content umbrella. Some readers might say that I'm killing any future chances I might have, to write for Demand Studios by publishing this and I would only respond in saying that I will never, at any point in the future, have any interest in writing for them. I will rather go my separate way, respectfully and wish them the best.

Approved for Rejection at DS

Some months ago, I submitted an application and a writing sample to Demand Studios (DS) and I was approved for a writing position. I noticed after approval, that they also have a blogger program, which sounded quit good (I publish a personal blog), although their description of the program was lacking in details. The program involves DS crawling your approved personal blog for new posts you have written and they will add those posts to the appropriate correlating DS website or they will add a headline to the blog-post on one or more of their sites. This increases their traffic and in turn, increases the blog owner's traffic as well.

Are Revenue Sharing Article/Content Publishing Sites Beneficial?

The sparse information they provided regarding the program also mentions presenting bloggers with the opportunity to earn advertising revenue shares over time.

Ironically, they reviewed my health blog and accepted it as meeting their standards for being well-written and active, with a professional appearance that they are seeking. At the same time, I was writing my first three articles for them, under the writer program, which I was also accepted into. These articles were in need of being approved as well, in order for me to be able to write additional articles for them. One of my articles was approved and appears on their eHow website. The other two however, were rejected, which stopped my ability to submit additional content to them, as an approved writer.

Excuses...Excuses...

When I submitted those first three articles and was asked by their editors to make a few changes within a certain time limit, I was undergoing surgical biopsies that very week and was very distracted by it and also by awaiting results on the analysis, which were to check for nerve damage in my leg.

Are Revenue Sharing Article/Content Publishing Sites Beneficial?

Some of the requests by the editor were reasonable, while some were a bit strange, with instructions for changes being written in such a way as to be difficult to understand.

My personal feeling is that the editor was in some way wanting to impress with technical language that did not make sense, rather than instructing with clarity. One friend I showed these edit requests to, who has far more knowledge than I in some areas of professional writing and from whom I have sought advice from on many occasions, stated that my instruction from the editor was badly in need of better explanation. Rather than request further ramblings from them however, I instead submitted enough changes that I felt would surely result in the articles being approved.

An Editor Scorned

The editor saw where I did not make a particular change they requested and when rejecting the articles they stated to the effect that I ignored one of their edit requests and their language made it evident that they were offended by this.

I will only add that some of what the editor referred to as not meeting guidelines, were in-essence, requesting that I not have any personal writing style included in the article. Some of the editor notes also stated that I was being too descriptive at certain points within the articles. This honestly makes me believe that some of the editors literally want instruction manual type articles that lack any personal touch to them. On the other hand this also likely depends on which editor is assigned over a writer's articles. I say this because I have since seen eHow articles with some personality from authors within them and many that do not at-all meet the type of standard this editor was seeking. Many eHow articles that can be found online, are very short in length as well, which I'm surprised does not send up a red flag to the search engines. I personally find it difficult to write an informative article that is also very short in length but this is obviously what the editors were requesting from me.

Rejected and Approved at the Same Time

Even with this having occurred, I kept my blog in the DS blogger program for several weeks following.

After a couple of months of observing what they do with one's blog I pulled mine out of the program. My reason for doing so is due to my perception of the program as being overly-beneficial for DS, with blog owners basically being avenues to further their conglomerate of websites. Amazingly, even with two of my three initially required articles being rejected by the editors at DS, they were accepting my blog posts for inclusion on some of their sites, such as eHow and LIVESTRONG.

The blogger program explanation on the DS site is simply too vague and I wrote them, asking questions for better clarification. Following below was my submitted message asking questions regarding the program, with their response to those questions, following below that.

My Questions to DS:

I have my blog in the blogger program and have some questions. I would greatly appreciate an answer to these, as they are not given detail on your pages describing the blogger program. - Thank You!

*1. When my posts are picked up by a site such as
LIVESTRONG or eHow, is the 1,000 page views
calculation based on the "Headline Views"
column or the "Post Views" Column, as posted in
my Work Desk?*

*2. Is there a way to actually view the posts that
are picked up from my blog and posted to one of
the DS sites (links to these are not shown in my
Work Desk)?*

*These questions are very important to me and
answers to them, will help me to know how
actively I will post on my blog (I may increase
posts significantly but would like to know what is
actually resulting from my blog activity).*

Thanks again

The Reply from DS:

Hi Jim -

Thanks for emailing us!

*When one of your posts' headlines is clicked-on
from a publisher website, that's what we qualify
as a "post view." These post views are what you
can generate revenue on. ---*

73

At the moment, headline views do not count towards the revenue share, as no ads are displayed along our headline widgets. From a quick glance at your account, it looks like you've got a few thousand headline views and a handful of post views.

As for viewing which posts are picked up, and links to them, we're about to roll out a new feature in the workdesk that will display this info! We'll be in communication with the bloggers about that (it's been a popular request). We're thinking this will be finalized within 4 weeks or less.

Thanks for being in the network!

Best,

The DMS Team

It was nice of them to send me these answers however; there are still a few unanswered questions. If for example, one discontinues with the blogger program at some point (i.e. they die, become ill or discontinue their blog), do the posts added from their blog, to DS websites, remain their property from that point forward?

They do require at least one new post per week on your blog, to remain in the program, so if a blogger were to miss posting for a month for unforeseen reasons, does this mean kaput!? No, there's simply not enough to go on, to know whether or not the program will actually benefit the blog owner in the long run and so I removed my blog from the program. This is not a choice that comes from my rejected articles with their Writers Program or I would have done so much sooner. It is based on what appears to be strange practices by this online conglomerate (i.e. not already showing links to where blog posts are being added and a lack of explanation for what the program entails).

Achieving Traffic for DS

I wanted to add that the headline views they achieved for DS sites, with use of my blog for the approximate 3 weeks it was activated in their system, was "13,394" views. These were shown to be coming from Livestrong, eHow, Computer Shopper, Chicago Sun Times and Answerbag 2010. Correspondingly, post views during the same period were "17" and clicks to my blog were "1".

At this rate, within a year or so of posting on my blog weekly, I might have actually seen 1,000 post views, while DS would have likely received clicks in the 100s of 1,000s within the same time period.

Chasing Off Legitimate Writers

I also want to add that I previously wrote for another very high standard content site with strict editorship and I had 117 articles approved within less than a year of writing for them. I also received two editor's choice awards for articles there and an editor complimented article as well. While it's very unlikely that Demand Studios would admit this, in some cases, their editors are causing writers who are potential assets to their sites, to be chased off by them or to be wrongly rejected.

Of course there are writers who are happy there and I say more power to them if it brings them satisfaction and fulfillment. You will also have those who can brag about the big dollar pay-offs they have received however, this again has much to do with which editors they have been dealing with, especially in regard to their first three article submissions.

Some writers, including me, look at the whole spectrum of content writing, including being able to place a part of myself into my articles (personal style) and while earning revenue certainly holds major importance -- it is not the only consideration involved for many writers who are passionate about their written works.

Extreme guidelines are great if the only objective is revenue but some of us enjoy a little more freedom and this is actually partly the reason writers are referred to as "freelancers". I have found by search online, where many formers writers for DS have made similar complaints to mine, plus many other types of disagreements being expressed regarding their practices.

In this case, I do not feel that DS is practicing dishonest business; they are however seemingly lacking respect for the personal writing styles of individual authors and they are not recognizing the apparent professionalism of others, whose work is being rejected by their editors. They certainly have every right to operate their content websites in any way they wish.

The negative press however, that has mounted against them and the high-potential authors who are staying clear of them as a result, is an effect that will either hinder their growth over time or they will remain unaffected and will continue to grow and to make an impact on the content revenue sharing website industry.

CHAPTER FIVE

A Content Site Who Deleted Contributor Articles with No Warning

(One More for My List of Negative Writing Experiences)

During my years as an author of online articles, which began in the year 2003, I have had both positive and negative experiences, producing content for websites. I recently contributed to a fairly well known content site, who suddenly deleted significant numbers of articles written for them by contract authors, for SEO reasons. The site I refer to will remain nameless, respectfully.

I recently became a contract member of this content website, where I was contributing to only one topic. The reason I was only writing for the one subject, was due to my feeling very wary of the website (a gut feeling I do not experience often). I will not attempt to say that this incident means that they haven't done good things for contributors but this particular event, I felt was not properly conducted by them.

It involved the sudden removal of many articles from their site that they felt were lowering their SEO ratings (Search Engine Optimization status). I was not the only member who did not receive an advance warning that our articles were being removed. In fact my email from them, explaining their decision for the content removal, came two days following my articles being removed when the topic they were posted under, was itself removed from their site (one that fell under religion and spirituality categories).

They did state on their forum following the action, that the removal was not based on quality of content (they practice strict editorial guidelines) and they were somewhat apologetic for removing it however, had some of the members, whose articles were removed, not backed up their work (saved to personal files), that would have been content gone forever for them. As you will see from my forum post below, which no longer appears at their site-forum, that the removal of content **was not** the issue but it was **the way in which it was done** that many of us, who were/are contract members of the website, disagreed with.

Like most people, I walked away from experiences like these and much worse ones, up until a few years ago when I decided that expressing opinions on these type issues publicly, helps us to learn from them. It can also actually help to change wrong policies in some cases and result in positive changes. It is my belief that wrongful activities can only grow, when people affected by them remain silent.

Following is the actual post I made, which was among many that other contributors also made in disagreement with the way in which our content was removed from the website:

My Post of Disagreement at the Content Site Forum (Since Removed by Me)

"In all likelihood, the administration will be deleting these posts but I for one will be saving mine and posting it elsewhere online. This website will of course find a way to smooth this over and anyone with administration will bend over backwards to defend what the site has done and may be doing soon.---

In fact, writers who aren't on the receiving end of this type thing will often defend a site as well, even in the face of obvious bad practices. It's like the saying goes -- "Whichever side the bread is buttered on".

*I have an interesting story in this regard and I wanted to add it in this thread. First of all however, I want to mention that the less-quality content sites have resorted to this type thing from the beginning. I believe writers literally begin believing at some point that **all** content sites want to bless them but in reality, their own businesses-online properties always come first. That's not to say that some content sites do not partner with their faithful contributors, because many of them do but some of them are overly one-sided in their own favor and in this type business, there has to be a degree of both give and take. Some sites resort to underhanded things to increase their revenue, at the expense of those who literally make their business work and prosper.*

This is not the first sour event I've seen at a content site and I could give other examples. ---

I will instead cite only one that this event has similarity to (regarding the lack of notice given) and that also indicates in my opinion, that the site is actually going a similar direction. The site I refer to is a "How To" property, who after gaining 10s of 1,000s of articles from authors, suddenly decided to cut off revenue sharing. Many authors raised a stink over it and over the fact that the notice for it was very inadequate. In fact many of us who wrote for them, did not receive an email at all (I had them remove my articles afterward but it took some pressuring). I received no email regarding this event that has occurred at this website either, in-fact I posted a new article today before I realized this had occurred (also taken down).

I've been in publishing for a long time, including about 65 books and e-books. I've written for many content sites as well and I can tell you with no reservation that the removal of the articles by contributing members was not a SEO based problem. For one thing the bulk of the articles have not appeared long enough to determine them to be lowering the site's search ratings. ---

83

If you'll note, other sites have these categories that were removed from this site and they have never once reported them to be a ratings problem. Some of my articles in the category that were removed get more traffic than do some of my health titles at these other sites (same topic -- not same articles).

Who knows why the site has done this but I will tell you this -- if they can resort to a mass removal like this, they are also capable at some point of other such practices. Their agreement does state that they can make changes, cancel memberships, etc... for any reason and for no reason, should they choose. Trust me when I tell you that MANY content producers have been burned by this type of thing and it also often backfires on the websites.

What is the future of this website? Who knows for sure but whatever it might be, it certainly will not include me. If only I had listened to my inward promptings, I wouldn't have invested the hours I did, creating those articles that were removed (many of you spent far more time than I did writing yours). ---

*I did save them however and I hope others did the same, especially those who had many. The fact of writers not having the forethought to back up their work is one major reason notice should have been ample on this action. It's almost as if they wanted to sneak it past as quickly as possible. **It's not** necessarily the removing of the articles but **the way** in which they went about it -- very improper...period."*

My post above, no longer appears at the forum of the website in question. I hold no grudge against them whatsoever but I do hope that my protest and that of the other members there will result in their giving better notice to members, when this type of change is being made, involving their personally authored content. (Note: Content producers can be dishonest and can commit unethical practices as well.)

To repeat: This and any other negative experiences I have had, does not prevent me from recognizing that good, honest content sites exist, in-fact, the one I refer to above is not necessarily dishonest but this particular action on their part was improper from any standard.

It also caused distrust by members there -- a fact that some of them stated in their own forum posts at the site, following the event but hopefully something positive can be learned from it.

CONCLUSION:

It is my hope that the preceding chapters help to give online publishers and authors ideas on how to protest or to bring resolution to issues that arise regarding online businesses they enter into contract with, who do not treat them fairly or who actually resort to dishonest and/or unethical actions that affect them negatively. It is also my hope that those who are involved with online publishing see the importance in thoroughly evaluating any online business opportunities they may be considering.

While negative experiences with electronic commerce can help one to learn valuable lessons, the best scenario would be to avoid them altogether whenever possible. This can often be accomplished by conducting online searches of companies and by observing how much information is revealed about them, on their own websites.

By taking these simple precautions, authors and self-publishers can increase their chances of entering into successful online publishing partnerships with reputable electronic commerce businesses.

(END)

www.ingramcontent.com/pod-product-compliance
Lightning Source LLC
LaVergne TN
LVHW042343060326
832902LV00006B/349